FOOTBALL: IT'S YOUR TEAM

Nate Aaseng

 Lerner Publications Company ▪ Minneapolis

To Gene Wickman

Manufactured in the United States of America

LIBRARY OF CONGRESS CATALOGING IN PUBLICATION DATA

Aaseng, Nathan.
  Football: it's your team.

  (You are the coach)
  Summary: The powers and responsibilities of a
football team owner are demonstrated when the reader,
acting as the owner, is confronted with ten different
situations that require a decision.
  1. Football—United States—Team owners—Juvenile
literature. [1. Football—Team owners] I. Title.
II. Series: Aaseng, Nathan. You are the coach.
GV950.7.A22 1985 338.7′61796′0922 [B] 84-23434
ISBN 0-8225-1557-1 (lib. bdg.)

1 2 3 4 5 6 7 8 9 10 94 93 92 91 90 89 88 87 86 85

CONTENTS

It's Your Football Team!

Your favorite football team just got pounded again last Sunday by a score of 31-10. That gives them four wins and six losses for the year. After four straight losing seasons, you're starting to get fed up with this. Who's to blame for this sad record, anyway?

The players can't help it—they're doing the best they can. Maybe it's the coach, then. After all, he's the one who makes all the decisions, isn't he? Coaches, though, sometimes complain that they don't have enough power to run things the way they want. The person with the real power, coaches know, is the owner.

An owner's decisions can make a team a champion or a loser. Successful owners seem to have a secret formula that keeps their team winning even when their best players and coaches retire. Other owners are like mad scientists who keep experimenting with new chemicals: no matter what they try, it all blows up in their faces.

Unless you have 40 or 50 million dollars in the bank that you don't know what to do with, you'll never own a pro football team. The next ten chapters of this book, though, will give you an idea of what it's like to be an owner. Your job is to build a championship team. It won't be easy. There will be times when you might feel like selling your club for fifty cents. Sometimes a single bad decision can send an entire city screaming for your hide.

What are you going to do when a coach quits on you at a key point in the season? How are you going to beat the other clubs in finding outstanding players? Is it smart to trade the best player on your team for a handful of draft choices? What will you do about free agents? It's your money; how much of it can you afford to throw around? As the team owner, you'll find problems coming at you from all sides. You'll have to deal with everything from lawsuits and angry fans to winter storms.

It's no wonder that many owners hire general managers to handle these problems. But other owners, such as Al Davis of the Los Angeles Raiders, prefer to run things themselves. And in all cases, the owner has the final say.

In this book, you have the final say. It's up to you whether your fans will get to cheer a winner or instead come to games with paper bags over their heads to hide their embarrassment. See how your decisions stack up against those made by real pro football owners.

We'll turn it over to you now. Every decision is crucial when it's your team.

1 How Much Is O.J. Worth?

You own the Buffalo Bills.

The 1977 season is finally over, and not a minute too soon for your Bills. It has been another disaster, with only 3 wins in 14 games. That gives you a two-year mark of 5 wins and 23 losses! The only possible excuse that fans have for coming to your stadium is to see O.J. Simpson. After nine years of thrilling sideline dashes and breakaway touchdowns, Simpson remains the top offensive star in pro football. Unfortunately, he can't win football games by himself.

Now the San Francisco 49ers have come up with a serious offer to trade for Simpson. They'd give a lot to see O.J. come back to his home town of San Francisco. You may never again get your hands on a player as good as Simpson. Can you afford to let him go?

7

O.J. Simpson turns on the juice as he tries an end sweep against the Minnesota Vikings. Could it be that the greatest star in your club's history is now trade bait?

Review Simpson's career with the Bills.

The 30-year-old Simpson suffered the first serious injury of his career in 1977. Because he missed half the season, he failed in his bid for a sixth straight season of 1,000 or more yards rushing. You never know how an injury will affect a player; it could be that O.J.'s skill will now start to fade.

Simpson appears to be healing well, however. He still has the powerful 6-foot, 2-inch, 212-pound build to go along with world-class sprinting speed. This combination has helped him gain yards at a faster rate than any other runner in the history of the National Football League.

After joining the Bills as the first choice in the 1969 draft, O.J. needed a few years to adjust to the pro game. But since 1972 he has been in a class by himself. That season he won the first of his four rushing titles with 1,251 yards. The following year Simpson sped to an NFL record 2,003 yards and averaged six yards per carry. In 1974, with O.J. carrying most of the load, Buffalo made a rare appearance in the play-offs. Fighting off the challenges of younger runners such as Franco Harris and Walter Payton, Simpson captured the NFL rushing yardage crown in 1975 and again in 1976.

Since Buffalo has not had a pro-level passing game for several years, they have had to rely on Simpson's long runs for almost their entire offense. In the past nine years, O.J. has contributed 10,183 yards and 57 touchdowns. Along with his warm smile and outgoing personality, his total domination of the Bills' offense has made him one of the most popular players in sports.

Now look at San Francisco's offer.

The 49ers will give you four high draft choices: second- and third-round choices this year, a number-one choice in 1979, and a second-round pick in 1980. Clubs with the worst records select first in the draft, and since the 49ers are a below-average team, that will give you a good shot at some very talented college players.

If your scouts do their jobs well, you might be able to get at least one star and two, possibly three, other starters out of those four choices. The trade would then strengthen you in four positions while sacrificing just one player. Another bonus is that you will be getting four young players in exchange for a man who may not have many years left as a pro. Simpson has already lasted far longer than the average NFL running back and may have a problem with that injured leg.

On the other hand, while the 49ers' offer looks generous, remember that they will not be giving you any proven pro players. Scouting is not an exact science, and every team has sad tales of the "can't-miss" college prospects who never played a down in the NFL. You may be trading a genuine star for a group of players who won't help you at all.

Even if you get lucky in the draft, it takes a few years for most college players to get used to the pro game. Since some of these draft choices are future picks, it may be five years before you get any use out of them. Can you afford to wait that long? With Simpson on your team, your offense scored only 160 points, the worst in the AFC last season. Without him, your offense may be so pathetic that fans will refuse to pay to see the Bills play.

1978 2nd Round Draft Choice	1978 3rd Round Draft Choice
1979 1st Round Draft Choice	1980 2nd Round Draft Choice

OR

What's Your Decison?

You are the owner.
Draft day is drawing closer and the 49ers are waiting for an answer. Are you willing to trade your star player for a bunch of "maybes?"
What will you do?

#1 Make the trade.

#2 Hold on to Simpson.

Make your decision. Then turn the page to find out what the Bills decided.

The Bills decided on choice #1.

It was obvious that after posting 2-12 and 3-11 records the past two years, the Bills needed a major shakeup. With a good deal of luck, skill, and effort, it would be possible to get the team back on its feet in two or three years. By then, Simpson would probably be ready to retire from the game.

So even if O.J. returned to his old form, he probably wouldn't be able to make Buffalo a winner. With that in mind, the Bills decided that San Francisco's offer was too good to pass up. Confident that they could get four top players who could help them for the next ten years, Buffalo saw the trade as a big step in helping them rebuild their fortunes.

Here's What Happened!

Two years after the trade was made, neither team was happy with the result. Buffalo's first two draft choices in 1977, Scott Hutchinson and Danny Fulton, did not break into the starting lineup. Within a couple of seasons both players were out of the NFL. The Bills then selected Ohio State linebacker Tom Cousineau with San Francisco's 1979 first-round choice. Everyone agreed that Cousineau would make a great linebacker. Unfortunately, Cousineau chose to do his linebacking in Canada, and he signed a contract with the Montreal Alouettes. Meanwhile, with Simpson gone, Buffalo's once-feared running attack ground to a halt, ranking last in the American Football Conference.

On the other hand, O.J. Simpson showed few signs of the talent that had made him the number-two rusher in NFL history. Forced to work behind the 49ers patchwork offensive line, Simpson took a pounding as he tried to find room to run. In two injury-plagued seasons in San Francisco, O.J. totaled 1,053 yards, far less than he used to make in one season during his glory days at Buffalo. That was enough for O.J., who announced his retirement at the end of the 1979 season.

Buffalo finally struck gold with their final draft choice from San Francisco. That 1980 selection turned out to be Auburn running back Joe Cribbs. An exciting open-field runner and pass receiver, Cribbs gained over a thousand yards rushing in his first two seasons and led the Bills into the play-offs. The Bills then made their trade look even better by swapping the rights to Cousineau with Cleveland. In exchange they received another number-one draft choice, who turned out to be Miami University's outstanding quarterback, Jim Kelly. It appeared that Buffalo had exchanged a worn-out running back for a young, All-Pro runner and a talented, young quarterback.

Thanks to the United States Football League, however, Buffalo had little time to gloat over the deal. Kelly signed with the Houston Gamblers in 1983 and Cribbs jumped to the Birmingham Stallions at the end of the 1983 season. In sorting through the whole trade, it turned out that Buffalo got three excellent seasons from Joe Cribbs in exchange for two mediocre seasons from O.J. Simpson. What could have been the steal of the decade for Buffalo turned out to be merely a good trade.

Shifty running back Joe Cribbs (above) spurred the Birmingham Stallions into the top ranks of USFL teams. Quarterback Jim Kelly (below) tore apart the same league in his first year of operating the Houston Gamblers' exciting run-and-shoot offense. Had Buffalo held on to these two, the Simpson trade would have been labeled a stroke of genius.

2 Can You Argue with Success?

**George Allen made the Rams winners.
Is he about to find out that winning isn't everything?**

You own the Los Angeles Rams.

There is a ticklish decison to be made this Christmas season of 1968. After three years of trying to get along with head coach George Allen, you have found that you really are not comfortable with him. You would like to find a different coach who suits you better. There are two problems, however. First, Allen still has two years left on a five-year contract. Secondly, he has turned your once-laughable Rams into one of the powers of football. Do you dare fire him?

Review what Allen has done in the past three years.

Considering all the trouble you went to to get Allen as a coach, it would look a little strange to dump him now. Back in 1965, your Rams could do no better than a 4-10 record, their seventh straight losing season. It was then that you lured Allen away from the Chicago Bears, where he was an assistant coach. The Bears hauled you to court, claiming that Allen was still under contract to them. Only after the court agreed with the Bears did Chicago owner George Halas mysteriously change his mind and let Allen go to the Rams.

Allen made the Rams a winner, and he didn't need a single rebuilding season to do it. With an 8-6 finish in 1966, he immediately brought the Rams the unfamiliar sensation of winning. By the end of the next season, he had constructed one of the finest teams in pro football. Led by his Fearsome Foursome on defense, Allen's Rams won 11, tied 2, and lost only one. Last year, he held steady with a 10-3-1 mark.

Allen also happens to be well liked by the players, especially veterans. They appreciate the confidence he has in older players, and they enjoy being on a winning team. The fans, too, are well aware that Allen is the one who made the Rams a power. They may not take too kindly to the idea of suddenly letting him go. Remember also that even if you fire Allen, you will still have to pay his salary for two more years.

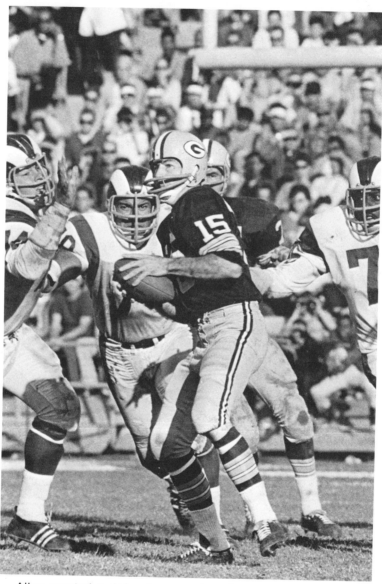

Allen created a defensive monster when he built his Fearsome Foursome defensive line. Unsuspecting Packer quarterback Bart Starr is about to feel the crunch from three of the
Foursome.

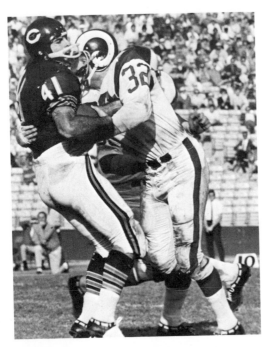

Two Ram veterans who have played especially well under Allen's coaching are Jack Pardee (32, top) and Myron Pottios (66).

Why would you want to let Allen go?

First of all, he's not the easiest man to work with. Although your problems with him are not major, you don't feel comfortable with him. Allen's system of relying on older players also makes you a bit uncomfortable about the future. What will happen to the team when these veterans get closer to retirement age?

There are rumors that Vince Lombardi is ready to get back into coaching. The coach of the great Packer teams of a few years ago is probably the most respected man in the game. Not even the most die-hard Allen fan will complain if you can get Lombardi to take charge of the Rams. The Rams, after all, haven't yet won a championship under Allen, and Lombardi is known for winning the big games.

What's Your Decison?

You are the owner.
It's the end of a season, and now is the time to make a change if there is to be one.
What will you do?

#1 Fire Allen.
#2 Keep him.

Make your decision. Then turn the page to find out what the Rams' owner decided.

The Rams' owner chose to fire Allen (#1).

Rather than try to work out his differences with Allen, the Rams' owner decided it would be easier to start fresh with a new coach. With luck, that coach would be Lombardi.

Every team in the NFL would love to talk Vince Lombardi out of retirement. The word is out that the man who drove the Packers to five titles in seven years during the 1960s is ready to get back into coaching.

Here's What Happened!

Allen, caught totally by surprise, did not accept the news peacefully. Although other good coaching offers were coming in, Allen wanted to finish the job he had started in Los Angeles. He appeared at a press conference along with an angry group of Ram players who insisted that Allen should be rehired. Several Rams threatened to quit if Allen didn't come back.

The outraged reactions of fans and the press rumbled through the Ram offices like a small earthquake. To make matters worse, Lombardi was no longer available for the job. You now have a real problem on your hands.

What's Your Decison?

Things have turned out worse than you expected. **Now what do you do?**

#1 Back down and rehire Allen. Let him coach as long as he continues to win.

#2 Stick to your decision and search for a new coach.

#3 Back down for now, and get rid of Allen when his contract is up in two years.

Make your decision. Then turn the page to find out what the Rams' owner decided.

The Rams' owner finally went with choice #3.

The decision to fire Allen had caused so much trouble in the Ram organization that the owner sat down with Allen to work out a plan that would help them work together more smoothly. By giving Allen two more years, the Rams accomplished two things. They saved the money they would have had to pay Allen for _not_ coaching, and they could wait for a better excuse to fire Allen. Perhaps in two years he wouldn't be so popular.

Here's What Happened!

With Allen back in control, the Rams won another divisional title in 1969 with an 11-3 record. The next year, the Rams slipped only slightly, to 9-4-1 mark. But after getting used to success, some fans were disappointed by the Rams' failure to get to the Super Bowl. When Allen was let go at the end of the 1970 season, the outcry from fans and players was not as loud as before.

George Allen then moved to the Washington Redskins and traded for many of his faithful, veteran Ram players. These players helped the Redskins win the NFL title in 1972, while the new Ram coach fell to a 6-7-1 mark. By firing Allen, Los Angeles may have blown a chance to get to the Super Bowl.

"Ramskin" middle linebacker Myron Pottios (66) continued to deliver hard hits such as this one on the Cowboys' Calvin Hill (35).
Next page: Another ex-Ram, Jack Pardee (32) wrestles Green Bay's John Brockington to the turf during Washington's championship season of 1972.

3 Starting from Scratch

You own the Toronto Northmen.

Talk about risk! You stand to lose a big chunk of your huge fortune if this new World Football League doesn't work. It will cost you plenty to put a team on the field in Toronto, and the odds are that it will all be wasted. You took on a tough challenge when you decided to compete against the powerful National Football League. They have all the top players and are getting millions of dollars from television networks. How can you get fans excited enough to pay money to watch your team?

Will high-scoring action be enough?

When the American Football League was formed in 1960, their players were far from All-Pro material. AFL owners made no attempt to sign star players from the NFL. Even if they could have interested some NFL players, few AFL clubs felt they could spend the money. Scrimping along on low budgets, they gathered those players who were considered too old, too small, too slow, or too clumsy to play in the NFL and added a few recruits from the Canadian Football League.

Since they had no stars, the AFL tried to shape the rules so that their game was more entertaining than the NFL's. That meant plenty of passing, long runs from scrimmage, high scores, and two-point conversions after touchdown.

Penny pinching helped the talent-poor league survive even though it attracted an average of only 17,000 fans per game during its first two seasons. And, while the crowds were small, the AFL's wide-open style of play won a large enough share of the television audience to keep them in business during the tough early years. Within five years, the AFL was on firm footing.

Should you try to outspend the NFL for college players?

Some football observers argue that what really saved the old AFL was a quick burst of cash. The New York Titans were being laughed out of New York and had to be run with league funds in 1962. Sonny Werblin then took over the team, which he renamed the Jets. His big move came in 1965 when he signed University of Alabama quarterback Joe Namath for an unheard-of amount, over $400,000. This shocking event brought the Jets lots of publicity as well as a fine player.

Similar signings by other teams brought more stars and publicity to the league. With these young players, the AFL attracted more fans to their parks and built fine teams.

Alabama quarterback Joe Namath (12) shows off his $400,000 arm.

Do you need to spend even more money to get NFL stars?

It's far more costly to start a league in 1974 than it was back in 1960. You may not have time to wait for fans to get slowly interested in your new league. Why not go one step further than Sonny Werblin and sign players who are already stars in the NFL?

There are three popular Miami Dolphins who might be interested in moving to your team. The biggest catch would be fullback Larry Csonka. His crushing runs won him the Most Valuable Player award in the latest Super Bowl. At 6 feet, 2 inches, and 240 pounds, he may be the most powerful running back in the NFL. Paul Warfield would be nearly as good a prize as Csonka. The speedy wide receiver has provided instant offense throughout his career, scoring 75 touchdowns and averaging over 20 yards per catch. Third man on the list is running back Jim Kiick. Although not on the level of the other two, Kiick is a capable runner and a good pass receiver.

Larry Csonka

Paul Warfield

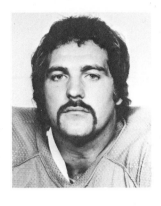

Jim Kiick

These three want to sign as a group; you take all or none. It will cost you plenty to sign them, perhaps three million dollars. Also, because of their current contracts, they won't be able to play for you until 1975.

What's Your Decison?

You are the owner.
It's your money that you're risking. Your brand-new team is up against the NFL.
How are you going to attract fans to your team?

#1 Start from scratch with average players but play an exciting, wide-open brand of football.

#2 Loosen up your wallet and go after top college players.

#3 Take a gamble and lure Csonka, Warfield, and Kiick away from the NFL.

Make your decision. Then turn the page to find out what the Toronto owner decided.

The Toronto owner decided on #3.

Well-known stars such as the three Dolphins would be sure to attract fans to the park. Fans would know that the owner was serious about putting together a top football team. The publicity from signing the three players might attract new fans as well. These Super Bowl champions had already proven that they could do well at pro ball and were therefore better risks than high-priced college players.

Here's What Happened!

While Csonka, Kiick, and Warfield were playing out their contracts with the Dolphins, the World Football League suffered through a disastrous first season. The Northmen were barred by Canadian officials from competing with the Canadian Football League teams and were forced to move to Memphis. All WFL teams lost huge bundles of cash.

When the Dolphin stars arrived in 1975, they were like three sandbags trying to hold back a raging flood. None of them enjoyed outstanding seasons, even against the weak opposition. Warfield caught 25 passes for 422 yards and 3 touchdowns. Kiick averaged only 3.8 yards per carry. Csonka was the worst disappointment, gaining only 421 yards on 99 carries and scoring only one touchdown.

WFL teams ran out of money so quickly in 1975 that some were unable to pay their players. Eleven games into their scheduled 20-game season, the league broke up. On top of all his other bills, John Bassett, Jr., the Memphis owner, was stuck with the enormous salaries of the three Dolphin stars, even though there was no longer a league for them to play in.

Bassett learned his lesson, though. As one of the founders of the next new league, the United States Football League, he settled for a more modest budget. While other USFL owners began throwing around millions of dollars for stars, his Tampa Bay Bandits built a solid team at less expense and enjoyed a much better start than his old Toronto/Memphis fiasco.

4 Surviving the Draft War

A Bronco uniform (white jersey) has not been something that players have worn with pride. Other than burning those striped socks, what can you do to gain the fans' respect?

You own the Denver Broncos.

Sometimes, though, you are almost embarrassed to admit it. Your Broncos are one of the weak teams that threaten to ruin the new American Football League in 1962. In fact, if it weren't for the equally bumbling New York Titans, your team would probably be the sorriest organization in pro football.

It won't be easy to build up your team. Your league has decided not to sign NFL players. Instead you will battle the NFL for the top college players in the land. You have to admit, though, that the powerful, established NFL has the advantage in going after these college stars. How will you survive in the NFL-AFL "draft wars?"

Look at what you are able to offer to a college star.

This is a case of the rich getting richer and the poor getting poorer. The best athletes will be more likely to sign with the best teams and make them even stronger. The short, sad history of your Denver outfit, meanwhile, may be enough to scare away top prospects. Who is going to be impressed with a team that posted 4-9-1 and 3-11 records in its first two seasons?

If they check further into the Denver situation, those stars will be even less impressed. The thousands of empty seats at your games are proof that the Denver fans haven't been sold on the Broncos as a major league operation. There are plenty of reasons for their doubts. The Broncos were so poorly organized that they used a football magazine instead of a scouting system to draft players in 1960.

Denver tried to cut corners everywhere to save money and they used ugly, bargain-priced brown uniforms and socks with stripes running up and down that had everyone giggling. They hired only two assistant coaches, fewer than most high school teams. Yet despite the tightest budget in pro football, Denver has been losing hundreds of thousands of dollars a year.

Don Stone carries for a few of his club-leading 505 yards in 1961. The number of fans in the stands shows that this is not a home game for the Broncos.

You have three possible ways of using draft choices.

You could draft the best players available and try to sign them. The Dallas Texans (soon to be the Kansas City Chiefs) are taking this approach. They are determined to get the top college stars to build a strong, young team and to attract fans. In 1961, they were the first AFL team to outbid an NFL team for a big-name player, linebacker-center E.J. Holub. The Chiefs have an advantage that you don't, however. They are owned by multi-millionaire Lamar Hunt, who can better afford to offer big contracts to college seniors.

Other teams such as the Dallas Cowboys of the NFL approach the draft more cautiously. Players who are drafted by both an NFL and an AFL team can choose which team to sign with. The Cowboys have a rule that they won't draft anyone unless they are quite certain that he will sign with their club and not with an AFL team. This policy stops them from drafting some outstanding players. But it costs them less money and it makes sure that they don't waste important draft choices on people who will sign with the other league.

If you don't want to bother with draft wars at all, you could trade your draft choices for veteran players now in the AFL. Teams that are at a large disadvantage in signing draft choices may want to try this. Although you would give up a chance at getting top young players, at least you would be certain of getting some capable players.

With your team doing as badly as it is, this may be the quickest and most certain way to improve your team. On the other hand, it's hard to build for the future when you are trading stars of the future in exchange for older players of only average ability.

What's Your Decison?

You are the owner.
Very few people are taking your team seriously. If you don't put together a respectable team soon, your Broncos may fold.
What plan do you have?

#1 Draft the top players and go all out to sign them.

#2 Draft capable but less spectacular players whom you are sure you can sign.

#3 Trade your draft choices for capable but less spectacular veterans.

Make your decision. Then turn the page to find out what the Broncos decided.

The Broncos decided on choice #1.

The chance to get well-known college stars seemed too good to turn down. Denver was convinced that the enormous cost of signing these players away from the NFL would be paid back by the thousands of new fans who would come to the stadium. If the Broncos could sign just a few of their top choices, they still might be able to build a winning team faster than if they only went after players they were certain they could sign.

Here's What Happened!

Denver's scouts did their jobs well. Four of their five first-round draft choices from 1962 to 1966 went on to star in the pros, and three of them went on to become among the greatest at their positions. Denver chose Utah State defensive tackle Merlin Olson in 1962, UCLA defensive back Kermit Alexander in 1963, tackle Bob Brown from Nebraska the following year, linebacker Dick Butkus from Illinois in 1965, and defensive lineman Jerry Shay of Purdue in 1966. Unfortunately, the Broncos couldn't sign any of them!

Olson became a key member of the Rams' famous Fearsome Foursome. Alexander gave the 49ers many fine seasons. Brown threw crushing blocks for the Eagles, Rams, and Raiders. The fierce play of Butkus for the Bears made him a legend. Shay signed with the Vikings and spent six seasons as a journeyman lineman in the pros.

Two of the fine players Denver lost were Jerry Shay (top) and Dick Butkus.

Had Denver signed these men they might have soared to the top of the AFL. Instead, wasting these valuable first-round choices kept Denver near the bottom of the standings for the next decade. It wasn't until the AFL-NFL merger ended the draft wars that Denver finally started to dig out of that hole. With no competition from other teams, they were able to sign running back Floyd Little, a first-round draft choice, in 1968. It wasn't until 1973 that the Broncos finally put a winning team on the field.

Charley Johnson, firing a pass over a 49er pass rush, finally brought a winning record to Denver in 1973.

5 Asking for Trouble?

Will swashbuckling former All-Pro Lyle Alzado give you more
headaches than he gives his opponents?

You own the Los Angeles Raiders.

You have learned that the Cleveland Browns are offering to trade their defensive end, Lyle Alzado, for a cheap price. Alzado is a tough, powerful veteran who was an All-Pro performer for the Denver Broncos in the late 1970s. His aggressive defense against running plays contributed to Denver's win over your Raiders in the 1977 American Football Conference Championship game.

It is 1982 now, and things have changed. After running into problems with the Denver management, Alzado moved on to Cleveland in 1979. Little was heard from him in the next few years as injuries cut down his pass rush. Alzado wasn't any happier in Cleveland than he had been in Denver. He now has the reputation of being an aging, outspoken, hot-headed, problem player.

Your club has had some success with older players whom other teams no longer wanted. It is worth picking up a player such as Alzado?

Look first at your previous success with "problem" players.

You've been lucky with several key players who were cut by other teams. Back in 1976, you signed defensive end John Matuszak. This giant 6-foot, 8-inch, 280-pounder seemed so wild and undependable that the Washington Redskins didn't even try to trade him in 1976. They simply cut him from their team in preseason. Matuszak then settled down to win a starting job with the Raiders and helped them to win the Super Bowl that year.

The next year, your Raiders added quarterback Jim Plunkett. Once a top pro prospect, Plunkett had lost his confidence and played so poorly for the San Francisco 49ers that they cut him in preseason of 1978. No other team wanted Plunkett, but you signed him and let him sit on the bench until he felt comfortable throwing the ball again. When starting quarterback Dan Pastorini broke a bone during a game against the Kansas City Chiefs early in the 1980 season, Plunkett came off the bench to lead the Raiders to another Super Bowl win.

John Matuszak (top) and Jim Plunkett were two "problem" players who turned into winners for the Raiders.

Now consider what could happen with too many strong-willed players on a team.

Your Raiders have been more fortunate than other teams in getting good performances out of difficult players. More often, rowdy players can make the coach lose control of his team. In 1972 the San Diego Chargers dreamed up the idea of stocking their club with hard-to-control players and with aging veterans. Tim Rossovich, Duane Thomas, Deacon Jones, John Mackey, Dave Williams, and Johnny Unitas were just a few of the players who streamed into the Charger camp. Exasperated teams were practically willing to give these talented players away. The Chargers then hired a psychiatrist in hopes that he could straighten out these players' problems and make them perform.

The result was a horrid mess that took the Chargers years to clean up. Instead of improving their record, the Chargers totally fell apart. None of the above-mentioned players lasted more than two years with the Chargers. The once-proud team had to start all over rebuilding their team and won only 9 of their 42 games between 1973 and 1975.

Even your Raiders don't have a perfect record when it comes to keeping players happy. Quarterback Ken Stabler and tight end Dave Casper were two free-spirited All-Pros who didn't see eye-to-eye with you and had to be traded.

Lyle Alzado

What's Your Decison?

You are the owner.
The Cleveland Browns are asking only a middle-round draft choice in exchange for Alzado, and your team could use a good defensive end who is strong against the run. **What will you do?**

#1 Make the trade for Alzado.
#2 Turn down the offer.

Make your decision. Then turn the page to find out what the Raiders decided.

The Raiders decided to make the trade (#1).

The Raiders have always taken pride in their role as the rebels and castoffs of football. Their owner felt that such players, if properly handled, actually make better players than those who always do what they are told. Alzado seemed to fit right in with the rest of the team. Middle-round draft choices seldom make it big in the pros anyway, so the Raiders weren't taking much of a risk in trading for him.

Here's What Happened!

Alzado proved that he was far from washed up. The emotional lineman took charge of a young defensive line and helped make the Raiders' defense one of football's finest in 1982 and 1983. Lyle's tough play at right end shut down opposing running attacks, including that of the defending champion Washington Redskins in the 1984 Super Bowl. For the third time in seven years, a castoff had helped bring a Super Bowl title to the Raiders.

Alzado (77) puts a bear hug on Washington's John Riggins in Super Bowl XVIII. The veteran end's play against 290-pound All-Pro tackle Joe Jacoby contributed to the Raider's victory.

6 Flying South for the Winter

Neither rain, sleet, nor snow keeps the Vikings from their appointed play-off rounds, but it makes it tough to practice.

You own the Minnesota Vikings.

Blowing snow, freezing winds, icy sidewalks! That's what your Vikings face when they try to practice for these championship games. It's 1973, and your team doesn't want anything to stand in the way of a Super Bowl title. After being embarrassed by Kansas City in Super Bowl IV, dropping first-round play-off games the next two seasons, and missing the play-offs altogether the next year, this talented, veteran team can't take much more frustration.

But you didn't look sharp in your play-off win over Washington. You need a good week of practice before taking on the Dallas Cowboys for the NFC title at Texas Stadium. Should you send your team south for a week of practice, or keep working out in Minnesota?

Consider what a trip to Tulsa, Oklahoma, has to offer.

The Vikings don't have much in the way of practice facilities, especially for indoor workouts. When the usual Minnesota winter storms blow in, it's hard for them to get the footing or the warmth to conduct a full practice. During this last week of December, you can bet on the weather being cold, snowy, or both. Snow is forecast for early in the week with cold temperatures following close behind.

Tulsa's December is usually much milder than Minnesota's. Tulsa can offer you an excellent practice field and is close to Dallas, where you will be playing on Sunday. Not only would you be able to go through full-speed drills, you also would be less likely to suffer injuries from slips on an uneven surface.

Another advantage in flying to Tulsa is that you will be able to get away from fans and reporters. Perhaps a quiet week away from the usual noise will allow your men to concentrate better on their assignments.

During the winter months, workers in Bloomington, Minnesota, prepare Met Stadium for use by removing the tarp—and the snow on top of it.

There are also good reasons to stay in Minnesota.

Disciplined coaches, such as your Bud Grant, worry about upsetting a team's routine. They claim that one of the reasons that Super Bowl games have often been sloppy is the way in which normal practice is interrupted during the Super Bowl week. The human body does not always adjust well to sudden changes. After months of practicing at home, working out in a strange place with unfamiliar weather for a week may have a harmful effect on your players. And while it may be nice to move into a quiet, restful atmosphere, it also might be a little depressing to be away from home, family, and friends during the holiday season.

Coach Bud Grant and quarterback Fran Tarkenton like to keep their team on an even keel.

Besides all that, it will cost money to keep an entire team in Tulsa for a week, and all of that comes out of your pocket. There is no guarantee, either, that you will find blue skies and warm breezes in Tulsa. Winter storms have been known to hit Oklahoma, and that would make the week a waste of time and money.

What's Your Decision?

You are the owner.
This is one of those nagging little problems that could actually decide if your team gets another shot at the Super Bowl.
What will you do?

#1 Go to Tulsa to practice.
#2 Stay at home.

Make your decision. Then turn the page to find out what the Vikings decided.

The Vikings selected choice #1.

Minnesota was in the middle of a bad postseason losing streak. When teams fall into a losing rut, most feel the urge to try something different. The Vikings were willing to part with a few dollars in hopes of getting some better practice conditions for their team.

Here's What Happened!

Thinking that they had left the arctic storms behind them in Minnesota, the Vikings instead found that winter had followed them to Oklahoma. They had barely arrived when a load of freezing rain and snow was dumped on Tulsa. The ground became so slick that the Viking team bus got stuck, and the players had to get out and push it out of trouble.

Although the weather warmed up quickly, it took another day before the slush, water, and mud dried up enough for the team to get in a decent practice. It seemed the trip would be a waste of money.

Fortunately, the Vikings were able to get in full practices the rest of the week. The weather reports from back home made them feel a little better. While the weather was clearing up in Tulsa, folks back in Minnesota were still shoveling newly fallen snow.

The break in routine hardly seemed to bother the team. In fact, Coach Grant gave credit to the peace and quiet of Tulsa for the team's nearly flawless performance that Sunday against the Cowboys. Led by brilliant performances from Chuck Foreman and the offensive line, the Vikings ran all over the proud Cowboy defense while the defense bottled up Dallas quarterback Roger Staubach. After their shockingly easy 27-10 championship win, the Vikings had to agree that the trip to Tulsa had been worth every penny.

The Vikings' week of practice in Tulsa prepared them perfectly for the Cowboys. Minnesota running back Chuck Foreman never looked sharper. Here he rips through the Cowboy defense for some of the Vikings' 203 rushing yards.

7 Terrible Timing

Surprise! Chuck Fairbanks' decision to dump the Patriots and instead join the University of Colorado has your players buffaloed.

You own the New England Patriots.

As you prepare for the 1978 play-offs, the last thing you want is a big fuss over the coaching staff. But that's just what you've got! Just hours before your final game of the regular season, head coach Chuck Fairbanks stunned the organization by announcing that he was quitting at the end of the year to join the University of Colorado. This has put your whole team in an uproar. How can you smooth things over so that your team can concentrate on the play-offs?

This may be the best Patriot team in history.

Your club is so loaded with talent that sportswriters are calling them the Superpatriots. They are about the only team in the NFL that can take on Pittsburgh's famed Steel Curtain defense in an honest, head-to-head battle and expect to come out on top.

The overpowering blocking of linemen such as John Hannah and Leon Gray has given you the league's top-ranked offense. They open huge holes for a host of runners such as Sam Cunningham, Andy Johnson, and Horace Ivory. Quarterback Steve Grogan is a threat to run or throw, and tight end Russ Francis gives him a huge, fast target.

On defense, you can unleash one of the fiercest pass rushes in the league on enemy quarterbacks. Add to that a talented group of linebackers, led by Steve Nelson, and young, hard-hitting defensive backs such as Mike Haynes, and you've got a solid defense.

With a team as powerful and talented as this, tricky coaching strategies may not be necessary in the play-offs. Just let them line up and play basic football and they should do the job.

Consider the effect that off-the-field controversies have had on your Patriots.

During the past few years, New England's record hasn't lived up to its talent. It seems that something is always happening to throw the team off stride. In the 1976 play-offs, the Patriots' anger at some questionable officiating affected their play as they blew a late lead against the Oakland Raiders. The following year, your team lost two early games while star blockers Hannah and Gray sat out in a contract squabble. Those losses knocked you out of the play-offs. This year's team has been missing some of its spark since wide receiver Darryl Stingley was paralyzed by a hard tackle in pre-season.

John Hannah

Finally, look at the situation that Coach Fairbanks has put you in.

You owe much of your success to Fairbanks. After coming over to the Patriots from a successful career at the University of Oklahoma, Fairbanks took a 3-11 New England team and within four years turned it into a powerhouse. Many of your players like and admire him.

Still, there's no denying that Fairbanks has stirred up trouble. Without any warning, the Patriots' coach of the past six years suddenly announced he was leaving. Even those who like Chuck are shocked. Others, especially the assistant coaches, are angry that he would bolt the team to get a bigger contract with Colorado. It's especially upsetting because Fairbanks has four years left on his contract, and therefore had no right to sign with another team.

The worst part of all, though, is the timing. How can Fairbanks keep his mind on the play-offs if he's also supposed to be recruiting for Colorado? And how can the players block out all this fuss so they can concentrate on getting to the Super Bowl?

What's Your Decision?

You're heading toward play-offs, and your head coach has just announced his resignation. Can you do something to get the situation back to normal, or will any further action on your part only make the situation worse?
What will you do?

#1 Keep calm and say nothing. Let Fairbanks keep coaching through the play-offs.

#2 Suspend Fairbanks until he guarantees that he won't have any contact with Colorado until the end of the season.

#3 Suspend Fairbanks for the rest of the year and sue him for not honoring his contract.

#4 Top Colorado's offer to Fairbanks and sign him to a new contract before the play-offs start.

Make your decision. Then turn the page to find out what the Patriots decided.

The Patriots went with choice #2.

New England certainly did not want the hassle involved with choice #3 at this important point in their season. They still wanted Fairbanks for a coach. Colorado's offer, though, had been extremely generous, and there wasn't time to try to work out a solution. Yet New England felt they could not let Fairbanks get away with what he had done (#1). The owner was especially concerned that Chuck would not be able to do a good job for the Patriots in the play-offs while he was preparing for the Colorado job.

The owner suspended Fairbanks before the team's final regular-season game at Miami and put two assistant coaches in charge.

Here's What Happened!

New England lost the game to Miami but still made the play-offs with their 11-5 record. Fairbanks, meanwhile, agreed to leave Colorado alone until the season was over, and he took over again as coach.

The Patriots were marked as the favorite in their first play-off contest against the visiting Houston Oilers. But it was obvious that New England was never quite able to settle down to business after their coach's shocking announcement. The powerful Patriots fell behind, 24-0, in the third quarter. Although they attempted a rally in the final quarter, they never came close to giving the Oilers a battle. Houston coasted to an easy 31-14 win. Both the Patriot offense and defense were unusually bad that day. New England's top-rated offense managed only 263 yards for the game, while the defense allowed an embarrassing 99-yard touchdown drive to the Oilers.

It was obvious that the Patriots had been unable to defuse the tense situation caused by their coach's action. Especially unfortunate was the fact that this was the last chance that the strong Patriot team had to advance to the Super Bowl. The team faded over the next few years, leaving fans to wonder what would have happened if the Patriots had been able to forget about controversy and play their normal game against the Oilers.

Houston's Earl Campbell
thunders through a gap
in the lackluster Patriot defense...

...leaving Coach Fairbanks to explain the embarrassing loss
to the press.

8 End of an Era?

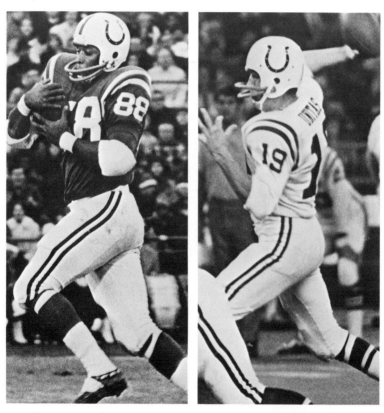

Can veteran Colt thoroughbreds such as John Mackey (left) and John Unitas still do the job, or is it time to put them out to pasture?

You are the new owner
of the Baltimore Colts.

Almost the instant you bought it, one of the NFL's proudest clubs turned to mush. The Colts, who rarely lose as many as four games in a season, have lost four of their first five contests in 1972.

For the last couple of years, the Colts have been described as a veteran team. But now some are convinced that those veterans are just too old to do the job anymore. Is it time to bring in some new faces and say goodbye to the Colt stars of the past?

Take a hard look at the Colt veterans.

These men are proven winners. Thanks to them, Baltimore has not had a losing season since 1956! Less than two years ago this team won the Super Bowl championship in a thrilling game with the Dallas Cowboys. They were still going strong last season as they put together a 10-4 record, good enough to make the play-offs.

The Colts continue to start one of the oldest and most experienced lineups in pro football. Quarterback Johnny Unitas, who was a star back in the days when crewcuts were in fashion, is now playing in his 17th season. He holds most of the important NFL passing records and is considered by many experts to be the greatest passer the game has ever known. If his accurate right arm is finally wearing out after all this time, you'd never know it by his last performance. Unitas threw for 376 yards in last Sunday's 44-35 loss to the New York Jets.

Other top performers from the past have had a little more trouble getting going this season. Among these are all-purpose running back Tom Matte, center Bill Curry, defensive end Bubba Smith, defensive back Jerry Logan, and ex-All-Pros John Mackey and Bob Vogel.

It was only a season and a half ago that these battle-tested
Colts claimed the NFL championship, thanks to Jim O'Brien's
last-second field goal in Super Bowl V.

If you look at the All-Pro selections of the last few years, it appears that all these people have long passed their peaks. Although several of these Colts regularly earned All-Pro honors in the 1960s, none has been named All-Pro since 1968. Still, they have continued to sport winning records. Can such untested youngsters as quarterback Marty Domres, running back Lydell Mitchell, and linebacker Stan White do any better?

Sooner or later friskier legs will have to be worked into the lineup. All-purpose back Lydell Mitchell hopes it's sooner.

Consider the danger in continuing to rely on older players.

The New York Giants put together a solid club in the 1950s and finished near the top of their conference year after year. As the star players grew older they seemed to get better. With veterans at nearly every position, the Giants earned three straight conference titles between 1961 and 1963. No one paid much attention to the worries of some that the Giants were about to collapse from old age. New York went confidently into 1964 with much the same lineup that had carried them to their last three titles.

All at once, the old arms and legs gave out. Quarterback Y.A. Tittle, flanker Frank Gifford, fullback Alex Webster, defensive end Andy Robustelli, and guard Jack Stroud all reached the end of their long careers that year. Safety Jimmy Patton, tackle Roosevelt Brown, and wide receiver Del Shofner hung up their spikes soon after.

With few new stars on the scene, New York crashed to a 2-10-2 record in 1964 and hit rock bottom with a 1-12-1 mark in 1966. Despite a few scattered winning seasons since, the Giants have never come close to rebuilding a championship team.

At the same time, consider what George Allen is doing with the Washington Redskins.

Allen seems to be proving that old is better in football. His Redskins are as ancient as the Colts, and look at them! With a 4-1 mark, they seem ready to challenge for the Super Bowl. Not only did Allen keep Washington's old-timers like Sonny Jurgenson, he traded for nearly every graybeard he could find. Jack Pardee, Myron Pottios, Richie Petitbon, Billy Kilmer, Ron McDole, and others are being called the "Over-the-Hill Gang," but no one in the league is playing better right now.

Down in Washington, George Allen is squeezing extra mileage out of his over-the-hill Redskins.

What's Your Decision?

You are the owner.

These early-season losses have got you worried.
What will you do?

#1 Stay with your popular veterans and hope they can pull out of this losing streak.

#2 Write off the season as a lost cause. Let your younger players gain experience and trade or bench the veterans.

#3 Gradually work younger players into the lineup.

Make your decision. Then turn the page to find out what the Colts decided.

The Baltimore Colts chose option #2.

The owner felt he could not afford to be patient. After such a poor start, the Colts' chances of making the play-offs this season were slim. It seemed a good time to try to find out what younger players could do. Sooner or later, the veterans would no longer be able to do their jobs. The Colts didn't want to wait until it was too late before starting to rebuild their team.

The Colts' head coach was fired before the next game, and the new coach was ordered to start young Marty Domres instead of the great Unitas. By the start of the next season, most of the Colt stars, including Unitas, Matte, Mackey, Curry, Smith, Vogel, Logan, Dan Sullivan, Fred Miller, Tom Nowatzke, and Eddie Hinton, were all sent packing.

Here's What Happened!

Baltimore's reshuffled Colts fell to a 5-9 record in 1972. As more new players were tested, Baltimore plunged to the bottom of the standings. Baltimore fans, who had come to expect success after so many winning years, were shocked and angered at the Colt management. It seemed to have been a horrid mistake as Baltimore won only 4 games in 1973 and were 2-12 the following year.

But it turned out to be a brief training period for a whole host of new Colt stars. Draft choices such as quarterback Bert Jones and the four members of the ferocious "Sack Pack" defensive line, Joe Ehrmann, Mike Barnes, John Dutton, and Fred Cook, quickly took over for the old-timers. By 1975 Baltimore had not only a respectable team but a divisional champion. The new Colts treated fans to three straight titles from 1975 to 1977.

The great Colt players who were dealt away turned out to be at the end of their careers. Within a year, almost all of them were out of football. In this case, the owner's sense of timing had been perfect, and his impatience paid off.

Next page: After brief, on-the-job training, Mitchell and his teammates brought the Colts back into the playoffs. Mitchell rushed for over 1,000 yards three seasons in a row and also led the NFL in pass receptions one of those seasons. Here Mitchell carries the ball in Baltimore's 1977 win over Oakland for the AFC divisional title.

81

9 Tug-of-War for a Tackle

A Texas shoot-out is shaping up over All-American tackle
Ralph Neely. The next move is yours.

You own the Dallas Cowboys.

There has been some dirty dealing in pro football in 1965, and you've been left with mud on your face. You just traded for the right to sign University of Oklahoma offensive tackle Ralph Neely, only to find that the All-American has already signed with another team. Neely is a valuable player who could fill one of your most urgent needs on the left side of the line. Is there any way you can fight back in this situation?

Think back on how this mess came about.

Your Cowboys had wanted to draft Neely but were unable to reach him on draft day. Since players who are drafted by both NFL and AFL teams can choose which team to sign with, you don't want to take any chances. Unless you talk to a player in advance and are quite certain that he will sign with you, you won't draft him. For that reason, you passed on selecting the 6-foot, 6-inch, 260-pound Neely, who was instead drafted by the Baltimore Colts of the NFL and the Houston Oilers of the AFL.

The Colts then found out that Neely was stubborn about wanting to play near his home in Texas. Realizing they had no chance of signing him away from Houston, Baltimore scrambled to keep their draft from being a total waste. They called you to see if you might be interested in trying to sign Neely. All the Colts asked in return for the rights to Neely was a fourth-round draft choice and reserve quarterback/punter Bill Lothridge.

Everything seemed set when you learned that Neely preferred Dallas to Houston. There was only one problem. Thinking that his only choice was between Baltimore and Houston, Neely had already signed a contract with the Oilers.

Houston's old pro, George Blanda, is looking forward to pass protection from Neely in 1965.

Can you ignore the Oiler contract?

Ordinarily, you would have to honor the Oiler contract. But both the AFL and NFL had an agreement with the college football officials that they would not sign any player whose college career was not over. Houston had violated that agreement by signing Neely before Oklahoma's final game against Florida State in the Gator Bowl. When it was discovered that Neely and some of his teammates had signed pro contracts, they were banned from playing in the Gator Bowl.

As a University of Oklahoma senior, Neely had no idea how complicated a pro football career could get.

What's Your Decision?

You are the owner.
Neely would really rather play for the Cowboys.
You must find a way to solve this problem.
What action will you take?

#1 Sign Neely and let the case go to court to prove that the Oilers had no right to sign him.

#2 Offer the Oilers a player or a draft choice for clear rights to Neely.

#3 Ask the commissioner to cancel the trade with the Colts and make them return Lothridge and your fourth-round choice.

#4 Avoid the hassle and costs of fighting for him. Admit that the Oilers pulled a fast one on you.

Make your decision. Then turn the page to find out what the Cowboys decided.

The Cowboys decided on choice #1.

Neely was a valuable player and the Cowboys refused to let him get away without a fight (#4). They were convinced that the Oilers cheated in signing Neely before the Gator Bowl and that the Oilers' contract with Neely was worthless. To the Cowboys, that meant that they owed the Oilers nothing (#2). Dallas wanted Neely much more than they wanted the players they gave up to the Colts (#3).

Here's What Happened!

Dallas announced that they had signed Neely on January 1, 1965. Since he preferred Dallas to Houston, Neely reported to the Cowboy camp and immediately won a job as starting left tackle. As expected, the Oilers brought the matter to court. While the lawyers argued the case for a year and a half, Neely remained with the Cowboys and helped them work their way to the Eastern Conference championship in 1966.

In November of that year, the Neely case was finally decided. The courts had determined that while Houston's signing of Neely wasn't exactly polite, it <u>was</u> legal. In the end, the stunned Cowboys were handed a stiff punishment. For the right to keep Neely, they were ordered to give the Oilers a first-round draft choice, two second-round selections, and a fifth-rounder. In addition, Dallas had to pay all the court costs involved.

The Cowboys protested that the arrangement was unfair. But that didn't mean that they thought Neely wasn't worth it. Big Ralph developed into an All-Pro blocker in his second season and was voted All-Pro from 1966 to 1969. He anchored the Cowboy left side for 172 games until he finally retired in 1978. During his 14 seasons, his steady pass protection and explosive run-blocking helped his team to two Super Bowl wins and four NFL championships. Although the price was high, Ralph Neely was, indeed, worth fighting for.

Ralph Neely gave the
Cowboys everything he had
—and then some.

10 Rent, Buy, or Goodbye?

"Vince" said, It's Not How You PLAY THE GAME It's IF You WIN or Lose!

Packer backers can't live on memories forever.
After years of frustration, they want victories and not excuses.

You own the Green Bay Packers.

Actually, you are not the only owner. The Green Bay Packers are the NFL's only publicly owned team. Like any large business, they have a board of directors to guide them. But you own a controlling interest and therefore have a voice in all the decision-making.

Your "Packer backers" are growing restless waiting for a return to the glory days of the 1960s. Here it is, 1983, and your Packers still haven't come close to getting to the Super Bowl since the days of Bart Starr, Jim Taylor, and the gang back in 1967.

Slowly, painfully, your Packers have built themselves into a contending team. They finally made the play-offs in 1982, and the team is looking to make a serious run at the championship in 1983. They had better, or the frustrated Packer fans will be howling for someone's head!

Wouldn't you know that a personnel problem would pop up when you need it the least? Defensive left end Mike Butler has announced that he's close to signing a contract with the Tampa Bay Bandits of the United States Football League. How important is Butler to your plans? Can you afford to let him get away, or is he asking too much?

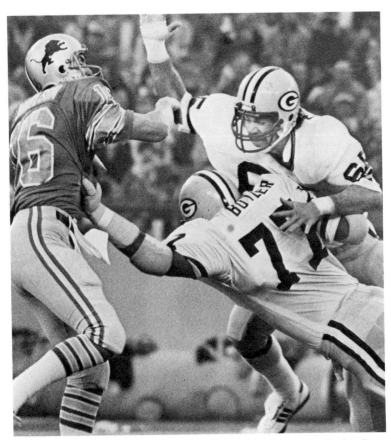

Butler, here making life uncomfortable for Lion quarterback Gary Danielson, has anchored the Packer defensive line since his rookie season of 1977.

Take a hard look at your defense.

Green Bay's explosive passing offense has hogged the headlines, but there are many experts who think the defensive unit is also first-rate. During 1982, your Packers clamped down hard on opposing runners and allowed only 3.4 yards per rushing attempt. Only one NFC defensive unit did better in that category. In a 28-team league, your Packers ranked a respectable 12th against the pass and a solid 6th against the run. Put them together and Green Bay finished 8th in the league in total defense, not bad for an "offensive-minded" team.

It all shows that Green Bay has gotten comfortable with its new 3-lineman, 4-linebacker defense. The linebackers, led by Mike Douglass, John Anderson, and Rich Wingo, storm around from sideline to sideline making big plays.

Mike Douglass   John Anderson   Rich Wingo

The defensive line hasn't won as much praise as the linebackers. The 6-foot, 5-inch, 270-pound Butler has always done well at blunting running plays. That has been especially important because most NFL teams prefer to run to their right, which is where left end Butler is stationed. But Green Bay's pass rush was little more than a pass trot last season. Out of the 14 teams in their conference, Green Bay finished 11th in quarterback sacks. Their lack of a pass rush also meant few opportunities for the defensive backs to intercept hurried passes.

Those who claim you don't need Butler point to these pass-rushing statistics. Since right end Ezra Johnson is known as a top pass rusher, it is obvious that Butler wasn't doing his share of hounding the quarterback last year. You are afraid that if you give Butler the salary he is asking, it would upset other players who were far more productive and are making much less money.

Think of your replacements for Butler.

Unfortunately, your roster is so thin in the defensive line that it's almost threadbare. If Butler goes, Ezra Johnson will be the only proven defensive end in camp. The two main candidates for Butler's job would be Byron Braggs, who has been around the league for several years without earning a starting job, and Casey Merrill, who has played well at times but is more comfortable at defensive tackle.

Ezra Johnson (90) demonstrates his pass-rushing power. With Butler (shown here above Johnson) gone, however, who will stop the run?

You've already blown a chance to draft some talented college linemen. Your Packers did not take a single defensive lineman in the 1983 draft until you selected Southern California's John Harvey in the 12th round. Even if such a low draft pick could make your club, Harvey was a tackle, not an end, in college.

In past years you could fill the weak spots on your roster with the final player cuts from the NFL's better teams. But this year many of those backup players have jumped at a chance to be starters in the USFL and are not available.

If you feel you can't do without Butler this year, you could sign him to a one-year contract. Even if he signs with the Bandits, his contract won't take effect until after the NFL season. That leaves Butler free to play for you in 1983 if you can work out an agreement. Such arrangements have been made in the past. Larry Csonka put in a solid year for the Dolphins in 1974 after signing a future contract with another league. It's possible, though, that with his fat USFL contract, there won't be any incentive for Butler to play hard for Green Bay. In that case, the Packers would be better off without him.

What's Your Decision?

You are in charge of the publicly owned Green Bay Packer football operations.

You're desperate to give your fans a champion-ship contender this season. Do you need Butler badly enough to give in to his salary demands, or can you do without him?

What will you do?

#1 Make an exception to your usual salary scale and top Tampa Bay's offer.

#2 Let him go to Tampa, but sign him for the 1983 season.

#3 Stick to your salary scale and say goodbye to Butler.

Make your decision. Then turn the page to find out what the Packers decided.

The Packers decided on choice #3.

The Packers were convinced that giving in to Butler's salary demands would cause more problems with unhappy players than it would solve (#1). They noted that even with Butler's "off year" in 1982, the defense was able to play well. With continued improvement from their younger players, they expected their defense would continue to improve, with or without Butler.

Although there was concern about the shortage of good linemen, the Packers decided against "renting" Butler for the 1983 season (#2). They felt that a player who had already signed with another team might not be able to give a true team effort to the Packers.

Here's What Happened!

It didn't take long for the Packers to discover that they had overestimated their defensive strength. Butler may not have been the league's best pass rusher, but he had more than made up for that with his work against the run. No matter who Green Bay tried to put in his place, opponents were able to open an express lane through the Packer left side. When the Packers later lost their top two nose tackles due to injury, their first line of defense crumbled.

Opponents stampeded through the Packer defense on long, time-consuming drives that kept the talented Packer offense pacing on the sidelines. Green Bay ranked dead last in the NFC in defense, allowing a whopping 400 yards per game. While the pass defense slipped to 12th of 14 teams in the conference, the once-proud rushing defense tumbled to 13th! There were no bright spots for the Pack defense as they ranked 12th in forcing turnovers and finished 11th in sacks despite 14½ quarterback traps by Ezra Johnson.

The powerful Packer offense fought hard enough to keep the team in contention for their divisional title. If it hadn't been for the total collapse of the defense, Green Bay would easily have moved into the play-offs instead of missing by a hair in their final game of the year. Could one man such as Butler have made the difference? The Packer braintrust seemed to think so. Their first two choices in the next draft were spent selecting defensive linemen to fill the spot left vacant by the departure of their big left end.

Although Green Bay's offense played like champs in 1983, the defense let their play-off hopes slide out of their grasp.

ACKNOWLEDGMENTS

Photo credits: Baltimore Colts, pp. 72 (both), 76; Vernon J. Biever, pp. 22, 52, 61, 75, 78, 94, 96, 99, 103; Birmingham Stallions, p. 15 (top); Buffalo Bills, pp. 8, 11; CAV/NFL Properties, p. 34; Chicago Bears, p. 41 (bottom); Thomas J. Croke, pp. 62, 70, 71; Scott Cunningham, p. 51; Dallas Cowboys, p. 93 (both); Denver Broncos, pp. 43, 44, 49; Green Bay Packers, p. 97 (all); Jocelyn Hinson, pp. 82-83; Houston Gamblers, p. 15 (bottom); Los Angeles Raiders, p. 47 (both); Los Angeles Rams, pp. 16, 19, 20 (both); Miami Dolphins, pp. 30 (both), 31; Minnesota Vikings, pp. 41 (top), 55, 56; New England Patriots, p. 65; Dick Raphael, p. 87; United Press International, p. 29; University of Oklahoma, pp. 84, 88; Washington Redskins, pp. 25, 26; Lou Witt, p. 37; Robert Wolfe, p. 4. Cover photo by Vernon J. Biever.

Also by Nate Aaseng

BASEBALL: IT'S YOUR TEAM
10 do-or-die dilemmas

BASEBALL: YOU ARE THE MANAGER
10 exciting championship games

BASKETBALL: YOU ARE THE COACH
10 exciting NBA play-off games

FOOTBALL: YOU ARE THE COACH
10 exciting NFL play-off games

HOCKEY: YOU ARE THE COACH
10 exciting NHL play-off and international games

COLLEGE BASKETBALL: YOU ARE THE COACH
10 exciting NCAA final four games

COLLEGE FOOTBALL: YOU ARE THE COACH
10 exciting bowl games

Lerner Publications Company
241 First Avenue North, Minneapolis, MN 55401

DE